Math
Yellow Pages

for Students and Teachers

Revised Edition

from the Kids' Stuff™ People

Incentive Publications, Inc.
Nashville, Tennessee

Special acknowledgement is accorded to

- *Marjorie Frank for compiling and organizing the materials included in this publication*
- *Susan Eaddy for the cover art*
- *Marta Drayton, Illustrator*
- *Jean K. Signor, Editor*

ISBN 978-0-86530-556-4
Library of Congress Control Number: 2001094393

7   8   9   10   12   11   10

Printed by Sheridan Books, Inc., Chelsea, Michigan • May 2010
www.incentivepublications.com

Table of Contents

SKILLS THAT MAKE A MATH WHIZ

Whole Numbers & Counting

_____ Recognize that numerals name numbers
_____ Associate word names with their corresponding numerals
_____ Identify equivalent and non-equivalent sets
_____ Arrange sets in order of size
_____ Count to 100 and higher (forwards & backwards)
_____ Count the union of two or more sets
_____ Skip-count by twos, fives, tens, and other intervals (forwards & backwards)
_____ Read and write numerals of 1-digit through 6-digits
_____ Read and write large numbers: millions, billions, and trillions
_____ Associate numerals with intervals along a number line
_____ Classify objects into sets
_____ Associate numerals with sets; write numerals to match sets
_____ Identify place value for 1-6 digit numerals
_____ Identify place value for numbers of 1,000,000 or greater
_____ Express numerals of 1-7 places in expanded notation
_____ Rename tens as ones, hundreds as tens, and thousands as hundreds
_____ Rename places of greater value than thousands
_____ Use whole number concepts in problem-solving situations
_____ Identify positive and negative integers
_____ Read and write Roman numerals
_____ Experiment with a non-decimal based numeration system
_____ Read exponential numbers

Number Concepts & Relationships

_____ Identify even and odd numbers
_____ Identify prime and composite numbers
_____ Order whole numbers
_____ Order integers
_____ Order fractional numbers
_____ Order decimal numbers
_____ Recognize ordinal positions (first through tenth)
_____ Recognize a whole as greater than any of its parts
_____ Understand the value of 0
_____ Understand and use the concepts of equality and inequality and the symbols =, < and >
_____ Compare numbers using words and the symbols < and >
_____ Complete sequences of whole numbers or integers
_____ Recognize and extend number patterns
_____ Describe relationships between numbers
_____ Round whole numbers to the nearest 10, 100, and 1,000
_____ Round whole numbers to the nearest 10,000, 100,000 and 1,000,000
_____ Identify and use number properties

Addition & Subtraction

_____ Learn sums through 20 or higher
_____ Use the terms addend, sum, and difference, and the symbols + and −
_____ Understand the inverse relationship between addition and subtraction
_____ Learn fact families through 20 or higher
_____ Recognize 0 as the identity element for addition
_____ Use the commutative and associative properties for addition
_____ Use a number line to find sums and differences
_____ Add and subtract vertically and horizontally
_____ Find sums and differences with 1- to 6-digit numerals
_____ Add and subtract with more than six digits
_____ Estimate sums and differences
_____ Check addition problems with subtraction and subtraction problems with addition
_____ Add and subtract without renaming
_____ Add and subtract with renaming
_____ Add long columns of numbers
_____ Solve word problems using addition and subtraction facts

Multiplication & Division

_____ Understand multiplication as the joining of equivalent subsets
_____ Understand division as the separation of sets into equivalent subsets
_____ Understand multiplication as repeated addition and division as repeated subtraction
_____ Recognize the inverse relationship of multiplication and division
_____ Use the terms factor, product, divisor, quotient, and remainder, and the symbols x and ÷
_____ Learn and use multiplication facts for factors through 10 or higher
_____ Learn fact families for products through 100
_____ Solve multiplication and division problems using a number line
_____ Recognize 1 as the identity element for multiplication and division
_____ Use the commutative, associative, and distributive properties of multiplication
_____ Understand the role of 0 in multiplication and division
_____ Multiply by a 1- to 4-digit number
_____ Multiply by large numbers
_____ Multiply and divide by 10 and multiples of 10
_____ Identify multiples of numbers 1–15
_____ Identify factors of a number; distinguish between prime and composite factors
_____ Complete prime factorization using factor trees
_____ Find the GCF (Greatest Common Factor) of two or more numbers
_____ Find the LCM (Least Common Multiple) of two or more numbers
_____ Divide by 1-digit divisors
_____ Divide by numbers of 2 or more digits
_____ Complete division problems that have remainders
_____ Use division to check multiplication problems and multiplication to check division
_____ Write and solve word problems using multiplication and division
_____ Find averages
_____ Determine if numbers are divisible by the numbers 2, 3, 4, 5, and 10
_____ Estimate products and quotients
_____ Select the appropriate operation for a given computation
_____ Find missing addends and factors in number sentences
_____ Solve problems with a mixture of operations

Fractions

_____ Use fractions to name parts of a whole or parts of a set
_____ Identify and understand the meanings of numerators and denominators
_____ Read and write fractions
_____ Add and subtract like fractions
_____ Identify multiples and least common multiples of two or more numbers
_____ Find the least common multiple for the denominators of two unlike fractions
_____ Rewrite unlike fractions as like fractions
_____ Add and subtract unlike fractions
_____ Identify common factors and greatest common factors of two or more numbers
_____ Identify fractions that are or are not in lowest terms
_____ Rewrite a fraction in lowest terms
_____ Identify and write equivalent fractions
_____ Compare and order fractions
_____ Identify mixed fractional numerals
_____ Identify improper fractions; rewrite improper fractions as mixed numerals
_____ Rewrite mixed numerals as improper fractions
_____ Multiply fractions
_____ Divide fractions using the reciprocal method
_____ Add and subtract mixed numerals
_____ Multiply and divide mixed numerals
_____ Use fractions to name ratios
_____ Express fractional numerals as decimal numerals
_____ Solve word problems with fractions
_____ Estimate answers to problems with fractions

Decimals

_____ Use dollar signs and decimal points to write money amounts
_____ Add, subtract, multiply, and divide money amounts
_____ Solve a variety of problems with money amounts
_____ Identify the value of each place to the right of the decimal point
_____ Identify terminating and repeating decimals
_____ Read and write decimal numerals and mixed decimal numerals
_____ Add and subtract decimal numerals
_____ Multiply and divide decimal numerals
_____ Learn to place the decimal point in products and quotients
_____ Solve word problems with decimals
_____ Estimate sums, differences, products, and dividends with decimals
_____ Express decimal numerals as fractions
_____ Express decimal numerals as percents
_____ Estimate answers to problems with decimals

Ratio, Proportion, & Percent

_____ Understand the meanings of the terms ratio, proportion, and percent
_____ Understand and write ratios
_____ Express ratios as fractions
_____ Express ratios as decimals
_____ Find and write proportions
_____ Use cross-multiplication to solve proportions or to find ratios
_____ Find percentages
_____ Express ratios as percentages
_____ Change percentages to ratios
_____ Use ratio to find equivalent fractions
_____ Use ratio to identify similarity
_____ Use ratios to find rate, time, or distance
_____ Use percent to find discounts, commissions, and interest
_____ Use ratio, proportion, and percent to solve word problems
_____ Solve word problems involving ratio, proportion, or percent

Problem Solving

_____ Identify information that is essential or nonessential for solving a problem
_____ Choose the appropriate operation(s) needed to solve a problem
_____ Choose an appropriate strategy for solving a problem
_____ Choose the correct equation to solve a problem
_____ Write and solve equations for pictured problems and/or for word problems
_____ Solve problems using information in charts, tables, and graphs
_____ Solve problems using information from graphics, illustrations, and maps
_____ Select and use the correct formula for solving a problem
_____ Estimate answers to word problems
_____ Solve word problems involving more than one step
_____ Predict outcomes in problem situations
_____ Solve open-ended problems
_____ Use mental math to solve problems
_____ Use trial and error to solve problems
_____ Use logic to solve problems
_____ Create a variety of problems
_____ Determine accuracy and/or reasonableness of solutions
_____ Give oral or written explanations of how a problem was solved
Solve word problems of various types, including problems involving:
_____ All operations with whole numbers
_____ All operations with decimals
_____ All operations with fractions
_____ Rate, time, distance, proportion, ratio, percentages
_____ Statistics
_____ Probability
_____ Time
_____ Money
_____ Measurement
_____ Geometry

Measurement

_____ Use the terms smaller, larger, greater, less and more to compare amounts and sizes

_____ Know the number of seconds in a minute, minutes in an hour, hours in a day, days in a week, days and weeks in a month, weeks in a year, etc.

_____ Tell time to the nearest hour and half hour

_____ Tell time to the nearest minute and second

_____ Use a calendar to identify, add, subtract, and count time

_____ Identify freezing and boiling points on Celsius and Fahrenheit thermometers

_____ Identify and use English and metric units for measuring length and weight

_____ Identify and use English and metric units for measuring capacity

_____ Measure length using English and metric measurements

_____ Measure temperature with Celsius and Fahrenheit thermometers

_____ Measure weights using English and metric measurements

_____ Measure liquid capacity using English and metric measurements

_____ Compare lengths, weights, and capacities of two or more objects

_____ Use a protractor to measure angles

_____ Measure the radii and diameters of circles

_____ Find the perimeters of regular and irregular polygons

_____ Find the areas of rectangles, triangles, and other polygons

_____ Find the circumference and areas of circles

_____ Find the volumes of space figures

_____ Find the surface area of space figures

_____ Find the capacities of a variety of containers

_____ Estimate measurements

_____ Add, subtract, multiply, and divide measurements

_____ Recognize the world's time zones; solve time zone problems

_____ Use a map scale to find distances on a map or globe

_____ Solve a variety of measurement problems

Coordinate Graphing

_____ Locate objects and points on a grid of 1–4 quadrants

_____ Use an ordered number pair to name the location of an item on a grid

_____ Place points and objects in a specified location on a grid

_____ Find locations using a map grid

_____ Locate positions on the earth's grid using latitude and longitude locations

_____ Graph ordered pairs of integers

_____ Graph solution sets to linear equations

Statistics

_____ Read and interpret tables of statistics

_____ Analyze data to find range and mean

_____ Analyze data to find median and mode

_____ Read and interpret bar graphs

_____ Read and interpret circle graphs

_____ Read and interpret line graphs

_____ Record data on a table or graph

_____ Construct graphs from statistical data

_____ Make predictions or solve problems from statistical data

Geometry

_____ Identify and draw basic shapes: circles, triangles, squares, and rectangles
_____ Identify open and closed figures
_____ Classify objects by shape
_____ Distinguish among different kinds of quadrilaterals
_____ Identify and construct parallelograms, trapezoids, pentagons, hexagons
_____ Identify and construct points, line segments, lines, and rays
_____ Identify and construct parallel and perpendicular lines
_____ Identify and construct intersections of lines
_____ Understand and use the term plane
_____ Identify and construct parallel and intersecting planes
_____ Recognize and name angles as acute, right, obtuse, and straight
_____ Distinguish between different kinds of triangles
_____ Identify and define corresponding, complementary, and supplementary angles
_____ Construct and measure angles
_____ Identify similar and congruent figures
_____ Use formulas to determine the perimeter and area of plane figures
_____ Identify the parts of a circle: radius, diameter, center, arc, chord, tangent
_____ Use a compass to draw circles
_____ Construct a bisector of a line segment and an angle
_____ Identify and construct space figures: cubes, prisms, pyramids, cones, cylinders, spheres
_____ Name and count faces, edges, and vertices of space figures
_____ Identify symmetrical figures
_____ Recognize and draw the slide, flip, and turn of a figure

Probability

_____ Determine possible outcomes of events
_____ Make tree diagrams to show possible outcomes
_____ Determine the probability of an event occurring
_____ Write a ratio to show probability
_____ Conduct probability experiments
_____ Determine probability for independent events
_____ Determine probability for dependent events
_____ Use the counting principle to find possible outcomes
_____ Describe the permutations of sets
_____ Identify possible combinations of sets within a larger set
_____ Determine odds "in favor of" or "odds against" the occurrence of an event
_____ Use probability concepts and calculations to solve problems
_____ Use random samplings to make probability predictions

Math Yellow Pages, Rev. Ed.

Pre-Algebra

_____ Identify opposites for positive and negative integers
_____ Give the absolute value for an integer
_____ Compare and order integers
_____ Add and subtract integers
_____ Multiply and divide integers
_____ Solve word problems and real-world problems with integers
_____ Describe relationships between numbers
_____ Evaluate mathematical expressions
_____ Identify terms, variables, and coefficients in mathematical expressions
_____ Simplify mathematical expressions
_____ Choose expressions to match statements
_____ Write expressions to match statements
_____ Choose equations to solve problems
_____ Write equations to solve problems
_____ Rewrite equations using inverse operations
_____ Simplify equations
_____ Identify and use properties of numbers and operations
_____ Solve one-step equations with one variable
_____ Solve multi-step equations with one variable
_____ Solve equations with two variables
_____ Solve equations with rational numbers
_____ Solve inequalities
_____ Graph inequalities
_____ Locate and plot ordered pairs on a coordinate plane
_____ Graph equations with two variables
_____ Graph solution sets to linear equations
_____ Identify transformations on a grid
_____ Identify corresponding points in transformations on a grid
_____ Graph transformations
_____ Identify and extend number patterns and sequences

GET YOUR NUMBERS STRAIGHT

Even Numbers — numbers that are divisible by 2

Odd Numbers — numbers that are not even

Prime Number — a number whose only factors are 1 and itself

Composite Numbers — all numbers that are not prime

Whole Number — a member of the set of numbers (0, 1, 2, 3, 4, 5 . . .)

Fractional Number — a number that can be named in the form $\frac{a}{b}$ with a and b being any numbers, with the exception that b cannot be 0

Mixed Fractional Number — a number with a whole number and a fractional number

Decimal Number — a number written with a decimal point to express a fraction whose denominator is 10 or a multiple of 10

Mixed Decimal Number — a number with a whole number and a decimal number part

Integers — the set of natural numbers (. . . –3, –2, –1, 0, 1, 2, 3 . . .)

Negative Integers — on a number line, all the numbers to the left of 0

Positive Integers — on a number line, all the numbers to the right of 0

Rational Numbers — numbers that can be written as a ratio $\frac{a}{b}$ where both a and b are integers and b is not 0 *(all integers and decimals that repeat or terminate)*

Irrational Numbers — numbers that cannot be written as a quotient of two integers (decimals that neither repeat nor terminate)

Real Numbers — rational and irrational numbers together are the set of real numbers

Opposite Numbers — two numbers that are the same distance from 0 but are on opposite sides of 0 (3 is the opposite of –3)

Exponential Numbers — a number with an exponent
(An exponent is a number written next to a base number to show how many times the base is to be used as a factor.)

Digit — one number in a numeral that holds a particular place

Significant Digits — all non-zero digits and zero when it has a non-zero digit to the left of it
*(The 0 in 4.03 is **significant**.
In 0.66, the 0 is not a **significant digit**.)*

Math Yellow Pages, Rev. Ed.

IMPORTANT PROPERTIES

Commutative Property For Addition
The order in which numbers are added does not affect the sum.
Example: 6 + 4 = 4 + 6

Commutative Property For Multiplication
The order in which numbers are multiplied does not affect the product.
Example: 8 x 3 = 3 x 8

Associative Property For Addition
The way in which numbers are grouped does not affect the sum.
Example: 7 + (3 + 2) = (7 + 3) + 2

Associative Property For Multiplication
The way in which numbers are grouped does not affect the product.
Example: (5 x 2) x 4 = 5 x (2 x 4)

Distributive Property
To multiply a sum of numbers, either (1) add the numbers in parentheses and multiply the sum;
Example: 4 x (6 + 3) =
4 x (9) = 36
or (2) multiply the numbers separately, then add the products.
Example: 4 x (6 + 3) =
(4 x 6) + (4 x 3) = 24 + 12 = 36

Identity Property For Addition
The sum of any number and 0 (zero) is that number.
Example: 7 + 0 = 7, 486 + 0 = 486

Identity Property For Multiplication
The product of any number and 1 (one) is that number.
Example: 9 x 1 = 9, 5840 x 1 = 5840

Opposites Property
If the sum of two numbers is 0 (zero), then each number is the opposite of the other.
Example: –4 is the opposite of +4 because –4 + (+4) = 0

Zero Property
The sum of 0 (zero) and any number is that number.
Example: 0 + 5 = 5 and 5 + 0 = 5
The product of 0 (zero) and any number is 0 (zero).
Example: 0 x 6 = 0 and 6 x 0 = 0

Equation Properties
When adding or subtracting the same number or multiplying or dividing by the same number on both sides of an equation, the result is still an equation.
Examples: n – 6 = 7
n – 6 + 3 = 7 + 3
n = 13

4n = 24
(4n) x 3 = 24 x 3
n = 6

MATHEMATICAL SYMBOLS

$	dollars		>	is greater than
¢	cents		≥	is greater than or equal to
Ø or { }	empty set		<	is less than
%	percent		≤	is less than or equal to
π	pi (3.14159)		≐	is approximately equal to
°	degrees		~	is similar to
F	Fahrenheit		≅	is congruent to
C	centigrade		≇	is not congruent to
√	square root		+ 4	positive integer
⌒	arc		– 4	negative integer
÷ or ⟌	divide		⟷	line
+	add		——	line segment
–	subtract		⟶	ray
±	plus or minus		∠	angle
X or •	multiply		m∠	measure of an angle
∪	union of sets		Δ	triangle
∩	intersection of sets		⊥	perpendicular
=	is equal to		‖	parallel
≠	is not equal to		a^n	a to the nth power
≈	is equivalent to			

CAN YOU SPEAK METRIC?

pico	p	one trillionth
nano	n	one billionth
micro	μ	one millionth
milli	m	one thousandth
centi	C	one hundredth
deci	d	one tenth
deka	da	ten
hecto	h	one hundred
kilo	k	one thousand
mega	M	one million
giga	G	one billion
tera	T	one trillion

Math Yellow Pages, Rev. Ed.

ALL KINDS OF FORMULAS

Perimeter

$P = s + s + s$	Perimeter of a triangle
$P = 2(h + w)$	Perimeter of a rectangle
$P = $ sum of sides	Perimeter of irregular polygons
$C = 2\pi r$	Perimeter or circumference of a circle
$C = \pi d$	Perimeter or circumference of a circle

Area

$A = \pi r^2$	Area of a circle
$A = s^2$	Area of a square
$A = bh$	Area of a parallelogram
$A = \frac{1}{2} bh$	Area of a triangle
$A = \frac{1}{2}(b_1 + b_2)h$	Area of a trapezoid

Volume or Capacity

$V = Bh$	Volume of a rectangular or triangular prism
$V = \frac{1}{3}Bh$	Volume of a pyramid
$V = s^3$	Volume of a cube
$V = \pi r^2 h$	Volume of a cylinder
$V = \frac{1}{3}\pi r^2 h$	Volume of a cone
$V = \frac{4}{3}\pi r^3$	Volume of a sphere

h = height
w = width
b = base
B = area of base
s = side
π = pi (3.14)
r = radius
d = diameter

MATH TOOLS, TREASURES, & TIDBITS

Handy Tools for Math Activities

abacus
alarm clock
attribute blocks
attribute cards
balance
calculator
calculator paper
calipers
cartons *(milk, cream, etc.)*
cash register
clocks
compasses
computer
counting rods
digital timers

egg timers
funnels
geo-boards
geometric plane figures
geometric space figures
globe
graduated beakers
grids
maps
mathematics glossary
matrix charts
measuring containers
measuring cups
measuring spoons
measuring sticks

measuring tapes
metric scales
mirrors
multi-base counting blocks
number lines
odometers
pegboards & pegs
protractors
rulers
scissors
slide rules
spring scales
stopwatch
thermometers
world atlas

Helpful Tools & Treasures to Collect for Practice & Problem Solving

bags
bank books
beads
beans
blocks
bottle caps
bottles
bowls
boxes
buttons
cans
catalogs
checkers
checks
clothespins
coins
containers
cookbooks

counters
cubes
deposit slips
dice
egg cartons
flash cards
games
geometric patterns
graph paper
jars
jellybeans
magazines
marbles
marshmallows
newspapers
origami paper
paper money
paper plates

pennies
pictures
pipe cleaners
popsicle sticks
posters
puzzles
recipes
rope
rubber bands
seeds
socks
stamps
straws
string
tangrams
tongue depressors
toothpicks
yarn

Math Yellow Pages, Rev. Ed.

SPECIAL MATH HOW-TO'S

How to round a number to the nearest ten:

If the ones digit is 5 or more, round it to the next highest ten (46 rounds to 50).
If the ones digit is less than 5, round to the next lowest ten (43 rounds to 40).

How to round a number to the nearest hundred:

If the tens digit is 5 or more, round to the next highest hundred (653 rounds to 700).
If the tens digit is less than 5, round it to the next lowest hundred (638 rounds to 600).

How to round a number to the nearest thousand:

If the hundreds digit is 5 or more, round to the next highest thousand (4,804 rounds to 5,000). If the hundreds digit is less than 5, round to the next lowest thousand (4,204 rounds to 4,000).

How to find an average:

To find the average of several numbers, add them together, then divide the sum by the number of numbers.

$$\text{The average of 12, 46, 75, 94, 101 and 38} = (12 + 46 + 75 + 94 + 101 + 38) \div 6$$
$$= 366 \div 6$$
$$= 61$$

How to determine if a number is divisible by 2, 3, 4, 5, 6, 8, 9, or 10:

A number is divisible by 2 if the last digit is 0, 2, 4, 6, or 8.

A number is divisible by 3 if the sum of its digits is divisible by 3.

A number is divisible by 4 if the last two digits are divisible by 4.

A number is divisible by 5 if the last digit is 0 or 5.

A number is divisible by 6 if the number is divisible by both 2 and 3.

A number is divisible by 8 if the last three digits are divisible by 8.

A number is divisible by 9 if the sum of its digits is divisible by 9.

A number is divisible by 10 if the last digit is 0.

How to determine if two fractions are equivalent:

Cross-multiply the fractions. If both products are the same, the fractions are equivalent.

$$\frac{5}{6} \approx \frac{15}{18} \qquad \begin{aligned} 5 \times 18 &= 90 \\ 6 \times 15 &= 90 \end{aligned}$$

$$\frac{2}{3} \neq \frac{5}{7} \qquad \begin{aligned} 2 \times 7 &= 14 \\ 3 \times 5 &= 15 \end{aligned}$$

How to tell which of two fractions is greater:

Cross-multiply the two fractions.

1. Multiply the numerator of the first fraction by the denominator of the second fraction: 2 x 9

2. Multiply the denominator of the first fraction by the numerator of the second fraction: 3 x 7

If the first multiplication has the greater product, the first fraction is greater.

If the second multiplication has the greater product, the second fraction is greater.

In this example, 18 is less than 21. Therefore $\frac{2}{3} < \frac{7}{9}$.

How to find prime factors:

Write every factor of a number.
Continue finding the factors of each factor
until only prime numbers remain.
A factor tree will help.

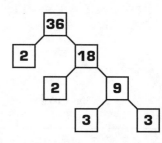

How to find the least common multiple of two numbers:

Write several multiples for each number. Look for the smallest number that is common to both numbers.

5 = 5, 10, 15, 20, 25, 30, 35, 40, 45, 50, 55

9 = 9, 18, 27, 36, 45, 54, 63, 72

For 5 and 9, 45 is the least common multiple.

How to find the least common denominator of two fractions:

Find the least common multiple of the two denominators.

For $\frac{7}{8}$ and $\frac{2}{5}$, 40 is the least common denominator.

How to find the greatest common factor of two numbers:

Write the factors for each number. Find the greatest factor that is common to both numbers.

The factors of 4 are 1, 2, and 4. The factors of 16 are 1, 2, 4, 8 and 16.

1, 2, and 4 are common factors. The greatest common factor is 4.

How to change unlike fractions into like fractions:

Find the least common multiple of both denominators. Remember the number you multiply each denominator by in order to get the least common multiple. Then, multiply each numerator by that number.

For $\frac{2}{3}$ and $\frac{4}{5}$, 15 is the least common multiple.

For $\frac{2}{3}$, you must multiply the denominator by 5 to get 15. So, multiply both the numerator and denominator of $\frac{2}{3}$ by 5. ($\frac{2}{3} \times \frac{5}{5} = \frac{10}{15}$)

For $\frac{4}{5}$, you must multiply the denominator by 3 to get 15. So, multiply both the numerator and denominator of $\frac{4}{5}$ by 3. ($\frac{4}{5} \times \frac{3}{3} = \frac{12}{15}$)

How to add or subtract fractions:

If the fractions have like denominators, just add or subtract the numerators (denominators stay the same).

If the fractions have unlike denominators, change the fractions into like fractions and then add or subtract.

$\frac{2}{7} + \frac{1}{2} = \frac{4}{14} + \frac{7}{14} = \frac{11}{14}$

How to reduce a fraction to lowest terms:

Find the greatest common factor and divide both the numerator and denominator by that number.

$\frac{24}{30}$ is reduced to $\frac{4}{5}$ when both numerator and denominator are divided by 6.

How to multiply fractions:

Multiply the numerators to get the numerator of the product and multiply the denominators to get the denominator of the product.

$\frac{4}{9} \times \frac{2}{11} = \frac{8}{99}$

How to divide fractions:

To divide a fraction by another fraction, multiply the fraction by the reciprocal of the divisor.

To divide $\frac{3}{10}$ by $\frac{2}{5}$, simply turn $\frac{2}{5}$ upside down and multiply.

$\frac{3}{10} \times \frac{5}{2} = \frac{15}{20} = \frac{3}{4}$

How to change a fraction to a decimal:

Divide the numerator by the denominator.

$$\frac{2}{3} = 3\overline{)2.000} \quad .666$$

How to change a decimal to a fraction:

Remove the decimal point and write the number as the numerator. The denominator is 10 or a multiple of 10, depending on what place the last digit of the decimal occupied. For instance, in .355, the digit is a thousandth.

First, write the fraction. $\frac{355}{1000}$

Then, reduce the fraction to lowest terms. $\frac{71}{200}$

How to change a fraction to a percent:

Divide the numerator by the denominator.
Then move the decimal point two places to the right.

$$\frac{3}{10} = 10\overline{)3.00} \quad .30 = 30\%$$

How to change a decimal to a percentage:

Move the decimal point two places to the right. 0.465 = 46.5%

How to find percent:

To tell what percent one number is of a second number, divide the first number by the second. Move the decimal point of the answer two places to the right.

For example, to find what percent 5 is of 20, divide 5 by 20.

$$20\overline{)5.00} \quad .25 = 25\%$$

How to find the base when you know the percent:

When you know the percent but not the base number, change the percent to a decimal and divide the percentage number by that decimal. For example, to find the base when you know that 76 is 80% of a number, change 80% to a decimal, then divide 76 by that decimal.

$$80\% = 0.8$$
$$76 \div 0.8 = 95$$
$$76 = 80\% \text{ of } 95$$

How to find simple interest:

Interest = Principal x Interest Rate x Time

Principal = the amount of money you borrow, loan, or deposit

Interest Rate = the percentage of the principal earned in a certain time

Time = the time period in which interest is figured

If $50 (principal) is deposited at 8% interest a year (interest rate) and left for three years (time), amount earned will be $12.00.

$$\$50.00 \times .08 \times 3 = \$12.00$$

How to find the probability of a single event:

The probability of something happening is: $\dfrac{\text{the number of favorable outcomes}}{\text{the number of possible outcomes}}$

A spinner has 3 equal sections, each of a different color (red, white, and green). If the spinner is spun once, the probability of the spinner stopping on green is $\frac{1}{3}$ because there is 1 green section, and there are 3 possible outcomes.

A spinner has 8 equal sections. 1 is green, 3 are red, and 4 are purple. If it is spun once, the probability of the spinner stopping on red is $\frac{3}{8}$ because there are 3 red sections and there are 8 possible outcomes.

How to find the probability of two independent events:

The probability of two independent events occurring is the product of their individual probabilities.

Toss a die and flip a coin. What is the probability that the coin will be "heads" and the die will land with 5 facing up?

Multiply the probability of heads ($\frac{1}{2}$) by the probability of the 5 facing up ($\frac{1}{6}$).

$$\frac{1}{2} \times \frac{1}{6} = \frac{1}{12}$$

How to find odds *in favor of* or *against* an event:

The odds in favor of an event = $\dfrac{\text{the number of favorable outcomes}}{\text{the number of unfavorable outcomes}}$

The odds against an event = $\dfrac{\text{the number of unfavorable outcomes}}{\text{the number of favorable outcomes}}$

In a contest, there are 10 boxes.
Three of them contain a $100 bill. The other boxes are empty.
A contestant chooses a box.

The odds in favor of getting a $100 bill are $\frac{3}{7}$.

The odds against getting the $100 are $\frac{7}{3}$.

How to bisect an angle:

1. To bisect $\angle$ ABC, place the point of a compass on point B. Draw an arc intersecting $\overline{BA}$ at X and $\overline{BC}$ at Y.

2. Use X and Y as the centers for two circles, and make the radius of each greater than half the distance between X and Y. Draw arcs intersecting at point Z.

3. Draw ray $\overline{BZ}$. Now there are two congruent angles, $\angle$ ABZ and $\angle$ ZBC. Ray $\overline{BZ}$ is the bisector of $\angle$ ABC.

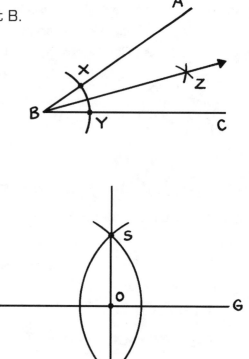

How to bisect a line segment:

1. Open a compass to a radius larger than half of the line segment you wish to bisect (here $\overline{FG}$.)

2. Use points F and G as centers and draw arcs that intersect above and below the line segment. (Here they intersect at points S and T.)

3. Draw a line which connects these two points of intersection (See $\overline{ST}$.) Point O is the midpoint of $\overline{FG}$, and thus $\overline{ST}$ is a perpendicular bisector of $\overline{FG}$.

How to tell if two triangles are congruent:

Two triangles are congruent if one of the following is true:

1. Three sides of one triangle are congruent to three sides of the other triangle.

2. Two sides and the angle between them of one triangle are congruent to two sides and the angle between them of the other triangle.

3. Two angles and the side between them of one triangle are congruent to two angles and the side between them of the other triangle.

How to find the length of the hypotenuse of a right triangle:

Use the Pythagorean theorem that gives the formula that the square of the length of the hypotenuse is equal to the sum of the squares of the lengths of the other two sides.

$$c^2 = a^2 + b^2$$

$$c^2 = 6^2 + 8^2$$
$$c^2 = 36 + 64$$
$$c^2 = 100$$
$$c = 10$$

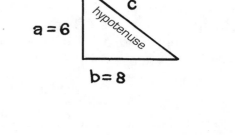

How To Make Your Own Tangram Puzzle

Chinese mathematicians invented a puzzle made from seven pieces. The puzzle pieces will fit together to form a square as shown, but the pieces also may be reconfigured to make many other shapes.

You can create different "pictures" by fitting the tans (tangram pieces) together.

This puzzle is 4 in. x 4 in.

You can enlarge it by copying it onto a larger grid.

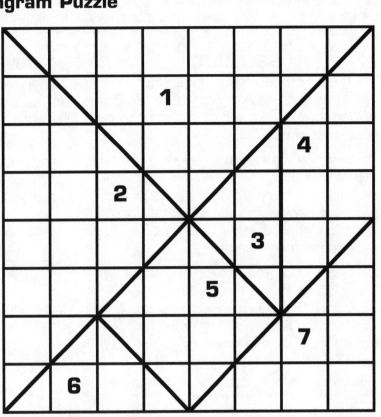

Try making some of these shapes using some or all of the pieces.

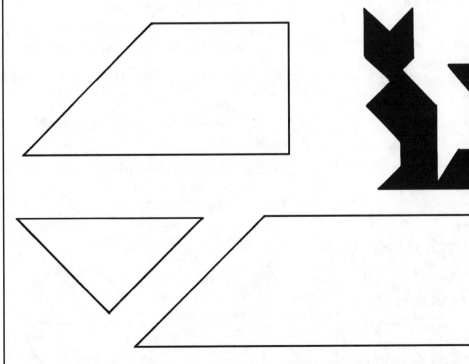

The puzzle may also be used to figure areas of shapes. Can you find the area in square units (without measuring) of each of the tangram pieces and each of the shapes you have made?

A HANDY GUIDE FOR PROBLEM SOLVERS

One of the keys to successful problem solving is finding a strategy that works for that problem. These strategies will help math students tackle just about any problem.

ESTIMATE

Many times you can figure out a solution by doing a rough or approximate calculation. This works well when you do not have to get a precise answer.

Maintenance workers want to set up several boxing rings in a huge sports center. They need a space 28 feet square for each boxing ring area. The sports center is 304 feet x 297 feet. Can they set up 15 boxing rings in the sports center?

Round 28 to 30. They'll need about 900 ft² (30 ft x 30 ft) for each ring. Then, round 304 & 297 to 300. The center is about 90,000 ft² (300 ft x 300 ft). You can estimate that there is room for about 100 rings (90,000 ÷ 900).
Then your answer is <u>yes, they can</u>.

TRANSLATE INTO AN EQUATION

In many problems, you have a mixture of numbers and words. It is helpful to change the whole thing into a number sentence.

The rock-climbing team climbed 200 feet on Saturday and 35 feet less on Sunday. On Monday, they climbed 41 feet more than on Sunday. How far did they climb all together?

This can be changed into an equation:
$$x = 200 + (200 - 35) + (200 - 35 + 41)$$

GUESS & CHECK

Sometimes the best strategy is to make a smart guess and then count or calculate to see if you are right. When you enter a contest to see who can come closest to the correct number of jelly beans in a jar, you are using this strategy.

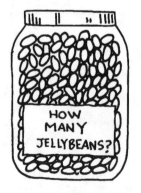

HOW MANY JELLYBEANS?

TRANSLATE INTO A PROPORTION

When the problem gives you a ratio and asks for a solution that is at the same rate, set up a proportion that will help you find the answer.

3 out of 16 skiers in the Himalayas claim to have seen the Abominable Snowman. At this rate, how many skiers out of 336 are likely to have seen the snowman?

Set up this proportion for this problem:
$$\frac{3}{16} = \frac{x}{336}$$
The solution is 63.

MENTAL MATH

Solve simple problems in your head. Often you do not need pencil and paper or other strategies.

It is 2:27. What time will it be in 3 hours and 30 minutes?

To decide what time it will be, mentally count 3 hours ahead from 2 P.M. (to 5 P.M.) and count 30 minutes ahead from 27 (to 57). The time will be 5:57 P.M.

TRIAL & ERROR

For some problems, you just have to try out different solutions until you find one that works.

The number of fans on the Booster Club bus is an even, 2-digit number. The digits are not the same. The sum of the digits is >10, their difference is <5, and their product is <34.

Try out 2-digit numbers until you find the answer to the problem. 48, 84, 47, 74, 65, and 56 are all possible answers.

USE A FORMULA

When you need to find a measurement, such as an area or volume, make sure you look up the accurate formula. To find the area of this circle, use the formula $A = \neq r^2$. You will find that the area is 113 in².

6"

DRAW A GRAPH, CHART, OR TABLE

Sometimes the quickest way to solve a problem is to create a quick graph, chart, or table to find solutions. This works best when you have statistical data that falls into different categories. For instance, if you must answer questions about scores in 4 different quarters of a basketball game, it will help to put them on a table or graph to get all the information in front of your eyes at once.

This graph can help you answer such questions as this:
Which team benefited the most from foul shots in the first 3 quarters?

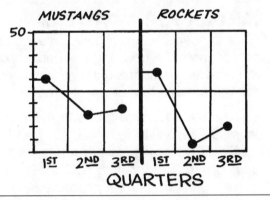

DRAW A DIAGRAM OR PICTURE

Some problems are just too complex to picture in your mind, so you need to sketch them out. A diagram will help with this problem.

A hurdler, gymnast, equestrian, archer, and diver have just lined up to buy lunch. The diver is the 2nd person behind the archer. The hurdler is ahead of the equestrian. There are 3 people between the equestrian and the archer.

Which one is at the end of the line?

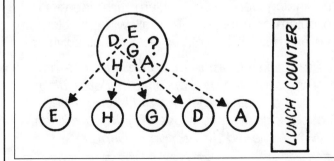

MAKE A MODEL

Create a model from paper, straws, blocks, or other materials if you need to visualize the problem to find a solution.

If you build a space figure with 8 faces, how many vertices (corners) will it have?

It will probably be easier to answer this question if you build a model out of straws and count the vertices.

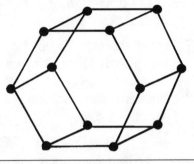

MAKE A NUMBER LINE

If you are adding and/or subtracting a number of facts, it might be useful to draw a number line to help with the solution. Draw arrows for each step of the problem.

Evan walks 1.5 miles on Monday, 2 miles on Tuesday, 2 miles on Wednesday, 0.5 miles on Thursday, and 3.5 miles on Friday. If it is Friday now, how far has he walked this week?

0 1 2 3 4 5 6 7 8 9 10 MILES

USE LOGIC

Lots of math problems need a heavy dose of reasoning, or logic, to find a solution. Logic involves using "If. . . then" thinking, where you say to yourself, "If this is true, then that must be true." You can use logic with this kind of problem:

Julie has completed more dives than Dylan. Dylan has completed more dives than Andrea or Thomas. Who has completed more dives: Andrea or Julie?

The logic problem is this:

If J > D and D > A, then J > A.

WORK BACKWARDS

Often it is helpful to start at the end of a problem and work backwards to find a missing fact.

Zak took a taxi home from the volleyball game. The cab rate is $4.50 for the first 3 miles plus .20 a mile after that. Zak paid the taxi driver $9.30, which included a $2.00 tip. How many miles was it from the gym to Zak's home?

Subtract the $2.00 tip. Next, subtract the amount for the first 3 miles. Then divide the remainder by .20. Take that amount and add the first 3 miles back on.

$$\$9.30 - \$2.00 - \$4.50 = \$2.80$$
$$\$2.80 \div 20 = 14 \text{ miles}$$
$$14 \text{ miles} + 3 \text{ miles} = 17 \text{ miles}$$

SIMPLIFY THE PROBLEM

Sometimes a problem can be made simpler by rewording it into a shorter or more straightforward question.

The coach makes the players run sprints for 15% of each practice. Practices are 2 hours long. How many minutes do they sprint?

Here's the problem stated in simpler terms: What is 15% of 2 hours?

CHANGE FACTS TO A COMMON ELEMENT

When you have facts that include different units, change the mixture into a common element—usually the smallest unit. Change yards and feet into inches. Change hours and minutes into seconds. For this problem, change gallons and quarts into pints. Then you can change back to larger measures, if you wish.

The team drank 12 gallons of sports drink. Jan drank 2 quarts. Samantha drank 3 pints. Amy drank 7 pints, and Drew drank 1 quart. How much did the rest of the team drink?

$$1 \text{ gal} = 8 \text{ pints so } 12 \text{ gal} = 96 \text{ pints}$$
$$1 \text{ qt} = 4 \text{ pints so } 2 \text{ qt} = 8 \text{ pints}$$
$$96 - 8 - 3 - 7 - 4 = 74 \text{ pints}$$

WEED OUT EXCESS INFORMATION

Some problems have information that is not needed. This excess information just complicates the problem. So it is helpful to be able to sort out what is not needed in order to find a solution.

Jenna's horse refused 4 jumps today, and cleared 12. Yesterday, the horse cleared 7 jumps more than today. She won 2 first place ribbons. How many jumps did the horse clear in the 2-day jumping event?

The information that is not needed is: the 4 jumps refused and the 2 first place ribbons.

LOOK FOR A PATTERN

Many problems involve an orderly arrangement of things or facts. Discovering the pattern can help you answer questions and find solutions. Look for the pattern in math problems.

Here are Carmen's race times in her first 7 races: 5:25, 5:21, 5:17, 5:13, 5:09, 5:05, 5:01. Here are Haley's times: 6:12, 6:05, 5:58, 5:51, 5:44, 5:37, 5:30. What will each girl's times probably be in the next three races? (Times are given in minutes and seconds.)

If you look for a pattern, you will see that Carmen has shaved 4 seconds off each race, and Haley has shortened each by 7 seconds. Once you know the pattern, you can answer the question.

RECOGNIZE UNSOLVABLE PROBLEMS

If a problem does not contain enough information, then it cannot be solved. When beginning work on a problem, first identify the problem or question. The following problem is an example of a problem that is not solvable.

The hockey team traveled on a bus in the snowstorm for 47 hours, 13 minutes after they left their hometown of Ontario. They had six delays and stops of 14 hours each. What time did they arrive in Denver?

WHICH MEASURE?

LENGTH

Metric System

1 centimeter (cm) = 10 millimeters (mm)

1 decimeter (dm) = 10 centimeters (cm)

1 meter (m) = 10 decimeters (dm)

1 meter (m) = 100 centimeters (cm)

1 meter (m) = 1000 millimeters (mm)

1 decameter (dkm) = 10 meters (m)

1 hectometer (hm) = 100 meters (m)

1 kilometer (km) = 100 decameters (dkm)

1 kilometer (km) = 1000 meters (m)

English System (U.S. Customary)

1 foot (ft) = 12 inches (in)

1 yard (yd) = 36 inches (in)

1 yard (yd) = 3 feet (ft)

1 mile (mi) = 5280 feet (ft)

1 mile (mi) = 1760 yards (yd)

AREA

Metric System

1 square meter (m^2) = 100 square decimeters (dm^2)

1 square meter (m^2) = 10,000 square centimeters (cm^2)

1 hectare (ha) = 0.01 square kilometer (km^2)

1 hectare (ha) = 10,000 square meters (m^2)

1 square kilometer (km^2) = 1,000,000 square meters (m^2)

1 square kilometer (km^2) = 100 hectares (ha)

English System (U.S. Customary)

1 square foot (ft^2) = 144 square inches (in^2)

1 square yard (yd^2) = 9 square feet (ft^2)

1 square yard (yd^2) = 1296 square inches (in^2)

1 acre (a) = 4840 square yards (yd^2)

1 acre (a) = 43,560 square feet (ft^2)

1 square mile (mi^2) = 640 acres (a)

VOLUME

Metric System

1 cubic decimeter (dm^3) = 0.001 cubic meter (m^3)

1 cubic decimeter (dm^3) = 1000 cubic centimeters (cm^3)

1 cubic decimeter (dm^3) = 1 liter (L)

1 cubic meter (m^3) = 1,000,000 cubic centimeters (cm^3)

1 cubic meter (m^3) = 1000 cubic decimeters (dm^3)

English System (U.S. Customary)

1 cubic foot (ft^3) = 1728 cubic inches (in^3)

1 cubic yard (yd^3) = 27 cubic feet (ft^3)

1 cubic yard (yd^3) = 46,656 cubic inches (in^3)

CAPACITY

Metric System

1 teaspoon (t) = 5 milliliters (mL)

1 tablespoon (T) = 12.5 milliliters (mL)

1 liter (L) = 1000 milliliters (mL)

1 liter (L) = 1000 cubic centimeters (cm³)

1 liter (L) = 1 cubic decimeter (dm³)

1 liter (L) = 4 metric cups

1 kiloliter (kL) = 1000 liters (L)

English System (U.S. Customary)

1 tablespoon (T) = 3 teaspoons (t)

1 cup (c) = 16 tablespoons (T)

1 cup (c) = 8 fluid ounces (fl oz.)

1 pint (pt) = 2 cups (c)

1 pint (pt) = 16 fluid ounces (fl oz)

1 quart (qt) = 4 cups (c)

1 quart (qt) = 2 pints (pt)

1 quart (qt) = 32 fluid ounces (fl oz)

1 gallon (gal) = 16 cups (c)

1 gallon (gal) = 8 pints (pt)

1 gallon (gal) = 4 quarts (qt)

1 gallon (gal) = 128 fluid ounces (fl oz)

WEIGHT

Metric System

1 gram (g) = 1000 milligrams (mg)

1 kilogram (kg) = 1000 grams (g)

1 metric ton (t) = 1000 kilograms (kg)

English System (U.S. Customary)

1 pound (lb) = 16 ounces (oz)

1 ton (T) = 2000 pounds (lb)

TIME

1 minute (min) = 60 seconds (sec)

1 hour (hr) = 60 minutes (min)

1 day = 24 hours (hr)

1 week = 7 days

1 year (yr) = 52 weeks

1 year (yr) = 365 or 366 days

1 decade = 10 years

1 century = 100 years

CONVERTING MEASUREMENTS

ENGLISH/METRIC EQUIVALENTS

English Customary Unit = Approximate Metric Equivalent

inch = 2.45 centimeters

foot = 30.48 centimeters

yard = 0.9144 meters

mile = 1.609 kilometers

square inch = 6.452 square centimeters

square foot = 9.29 square centimeters

square yard = 0.836 square meters

square mile = 2.590 square kilometers

acre = 4047 square meters

cubic inch = 16.387 cubic centimeters

cubic foot = 28,317 cubic centimeters

cubic yard = 0.765 cubic meters

ounce = 28.3495 grams

pound = 453.59 grams

ton = 907.18 kilograms

pint = 0.4732 liters

quart = 0.9465 liters

gallon = 3.785 liters

bushel = 35.2390 liters

FROM METRIC TO ENGLISH

To change centimeters	to inches	multiply by 0.3937
To change meters	to feet	multiply by 3.2808
To change kilometers	to miles	multiply by 0.6214
To change liters	to quarts	multiply by 1.0567
To change kilograms	to pounds	multiply by 2.2046
To change metric tons	to English tons	multiply by 1.1023

TEMPERATURE CONVERSIONS

To change Fahrenheit to Celsius: subtract 32, then multiply by $\frac{5}{9}$

To change Celsius to Fahrenheit: multiply by $\frac{9}{5}$, then add 32

TRICKS FOR MATHEMATICIANS

The 3–Digit Trick

1. Write any 3 digits.   472

2. Repeat the numbers in the same order
   to get a 6-digit number.   472,472

3. Divide the 6-digit number by 13.

$$\begin{array}{r} 36{,}344 \\ 13\overline{)472{,}472} \end{array}$$

4. Divide the resulting number by 11.

$$\begin{array}{r} 3{,}304 \\ 11\overline{)36{,}344} \end{array}$$

5. Divide the resulting number by 7.

$$\begin{array}{r} 472 \\ 7\overline{)3{,}304} \end{array}$$

The final answer will always be the original number.   472

A Fancy Number Pattern

1. Write any four digits, repeating the
   first digit at the end for a total of five
   digits in a row.

2. Subtract to find the difference between
   each pair of digits, then write each
   answer below that pair of digits.
   Always repeat the first digit of each
   row at the end of that row.

3. Continue in this manner until you get a
   row of the same numbers. It will work
   every time with any group of numbers!

```
2   6   8   9   2
  4   2   1   7   4
    2   1   6   3   2
      1   5   3   1   1
        4   2   2   0   4
          2   0   2   4   2
            2   2   2   2   2
```

Goldbach's Guesses

A man named Christian Goldbach made these two "guesses" (theories) in 1742. No one has ever been able to prove that either is always true, but no one has ever found a case in which either is false. Experiment with them on your own.

Every even number greater than 2 is the sum of two prime numbers.

$$6 = 1 + 5$$

Every odd number greater than 7 is the sum of three prime numbers.

$$17 = 5 + 5 + 7$$

Math Yellow Pages, Rev. Ed.

The Palindrome Trick

A palindrome is a number that reads the same forward and backward, such as 48,784. There is a trick to finding palindromes. Follow the steps below.

1. Write a number.

2. Reverse the number and add.

3. Continue this process until you get a palindrome.

```
    597
 + 795
   1392
 + 2931
   4323
 + 3234
   7557
```

The Reappearing Number Trick

Ask a friend to choose any four digits and follow these directions. The same number will appear every time.

1. Choose four different digits from 0 to 9.

       1572

2. Arrange the numbers to make the largest possible number.
   Arrange the numbers again to make the smallest possible number.
   Subtract the smaller number from the larger number.

```
   7521
 - 1257
   6264
```

3. Arrange the individual numbers in the resulting answer to make the largest and smallest possible numbers.
   Subtract the numbers as before.

```
   6642
 - 2466
   4176
```

4. Continue the process in the same manner.
   Eventually you will arrive at the number 6174.
   No matter what four numbers you choose,
   the number 6174 will always appear!

```
   7641
 - 1467
   6174
```

Pascal's Tricky Triangle

Blaise Pascal, a famous French mathematician, discovered this unique triangle. Look carefully at the numbers and try to discover the secret pattern.

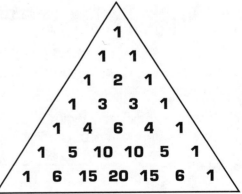

- Add each row across. Notice the pattern of the sums.

- Add each diagonal row from right to left. Notice the pattern of the sums.

- Add each diagonal row from left to right. Notice the pattern of the sums.

(The main secret of the triangle is that each number is the sum of the two numbers above it.)

Magic Squares

Whether adding the rows down, up, across, or diagonally, all of the sums are the same in a magic square.

After adding the rows in this magic square, you will discover that every sum is 15.

8	3	4
1	5	9
6	7	2

Fill in the missing numbers to make each of these a magic square.

5	8	
6	6	6
	4	7

6		6
	7	7
8		8

0	4	8
	6	

Try making your own magic squares!

A Multiplication Trick

Here's a fun way to check multiplication problems.

The problem:

1. First, work the problem and write the answer. ⟶ 3752 x 1608 = 6,033,216

2. Then add the digits in each factor. ⟶ 3 + 7 + 5 + 2 = 17
   1 + 6 + 0 + 8 = 15

3. Now add the digits in each answer of step 2. ⟶ 1 + 7 = 8
   1 + 5 = 6

4. Multiply the two answers from step 3. ⟶ 8 x 6 = 48

5. Add the digits in the product. Continue adding the digits in the resulting answers until you get a 1-digit answer. ⟶ 4 + 8 = 12
   1 + 2 = 3

• • • • •

6. Now add the digits in the product of the original problem. ⟶ 6 + 0 + 3 + 3 + 2 + 1 + 6 = 21

7. Continue adding the digits in the resulting answers until you get a 1-digit answer. ⟶ 2 + 1 = 3

8. If both 1-digit answers (step 5 and step 7) are the same, the product of the problem is correct. (If the problem was not done correctly to begin with, these last two numbers will not match.) ⟶ 3 = 3

COMPUTER TALK

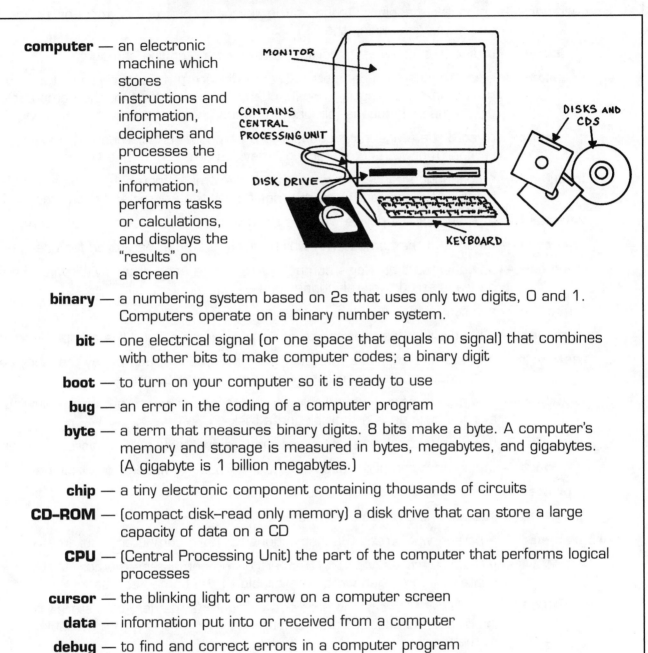

computer — an electronic machine which stores instructions and information, deciphers and processes the instructions and information, performs tasks or calculations, and displays the "results" on a screen

MONITOR

CONTAINS CENTRAL PROCESSING UNIT

DISK DRIVE

DISKS AND CDS

KEYBOARD

binary — a numbering system based on 2s that uses only two digits, O and 1. Computers operate on a binary number system.

bit — one electrical signal (or one space that equals no signal) that combines with other bits to make computer codes; a binary digit

boot — to turn on your computer so it is ready to use

bug — an error in the coding of a computer program

byte — a term that measures binary digits. 8 bits make a byte. A computer's memory and storage is measured in bytes, megabytes, and gigabytes. (A gigabyte is 1 billion megabytes.)

chip — a tiny electronic component containing thousands of circuits

CD–ROM — (compact disk–read only memory) a disk drive that can store a large capacity of data on a CD

CPU — (Central Processing Unit) the part of the computer that performs logical processes

cursor — the blinking light or arrow on a computer screen

data — information put into or received from a computer

debug — to find and correct errors in a computer program

desktop — the programs that you keep on your computer, usually represented by icons on an opening screen

disk drive — a device in or attached to the computer which reads information from disks, and writes information onto disks

file — a group of related data on a computer that is the electronic description of a document, picture, program, or other object

floppy disk — a plastic disk, separate from the computer, that can be inserted into a slot on the computer to transfer data so it can be stored outside the computer

hard disk — a permanent part of the computer that stores data

hard drive — the computer unit containing the hard disk and other instruments to read and write data

hardware — computer machinery (such as the keyboard, disk drives, monitor, printer, and device containing the CPU)

install — to set up a software program so that it runs on the computer

icons — small images on a computer screen that are the visual representation of the computer's programs or functions, or connections to the computer's programs or functions (clicking on an icon opens or activates the program)

input — to enter data and instructions into a computer either manually (with a keyboard) or with computer input devices other than a keyboard

interface — a connection between two computer systems or computer devices (such as between the keyboard and the monitor, or the printer and the computer)

keyboard — a typewriter-like device which is used to type information into the computer

memory — an area of the computer in which information can be stored for use

modem — a connector that allows computers to talk to each other by allowing data to be transferred over telephone lines

monitor — a screen which displays information

mouse — a hand-guided device used to move the cursor around the computer screen

network — a group of computers that are joined together in such a way that they can share data and supplementary equipment such as printers

output — information a computer displays on a screen or prints out after following a set of instructions or completing a task

PC — acronym (short name) for a personal computer, usually a microcomputer

port — a plug on a computer used to attach a mouse, modem, or other device

printer — a machine for printing output

program — instructions given to a computer

programmer — a person who writes the instructions to make computer programs run

RAM — *(Random Access Memory)* the part of the computer's memory that contains information which is available to the computer's user

ROM — *(Read Only Memory)* the part of a computer's memory that stores information needed for the computer to work properly (not available to the user)

scanner — a device used to make a copy of a picture that a computer can read

scrolling — using arrow keys or the mouse to move images or text on the screen up or down

software — computer programs which enable computers to carry out tasks. Software is found on disks, tapes, or cards, or it can be downloaded from the Internet.

terminal — a device for displaying input and output, usually located separately from the computer itself and generally consisting of a keyboard and monitor

virus — a "bug" or program that interrupts normal functioning of your computer's software or hardware

zip — to make a file smaller by compressing it

WEB TALK

analog signals — signals that can travel along telephone lines

baud — a unit used to measure the speed at which a modem transfers data

bookmark — a shortcut option that keeps track of a site you have already visited and allows you to visit again without typing in the address

BPS — *(Bits Per Second)* how fast information moves from one place to another

browser — a software tool that is used to view sites on the Internet

chatting — "talking" with other people on the Internet (usually by typing)

chat rooms — *(or chat groups)* addresses online where many people can talk to each other at one time

cookie — little bits of text or code that a web server leaves on your computer to track information about your personal preferences

cyberspace — refers to all the resources available on the Internet, or the "place" out there where people and ideas meet on the Internet

digital signal — electrical signals that travel through a computer

discussion group — a group of people who get together on the web to talk about a certain topic

domain name — the name that identifies an Internet site

download — to copy files or programs or information from Internet sites

email — *(electronic mail)* mail that is sent over the Internet between computers

encryption — a complicated code used to keep information secret

FAQs — *(Frequently Asked Questions)* answers to questions asked frequently in a particular website or discussion group

fiber optic cable — a way to connect to the Internet that transfers data much faster than telephone cable

FTP — *(File Transfer Protocol)* rules of a system used to transfer certain types of files over the Internet

GIF — *(Graphics Interchange Format)* a graphics file format frequently used to display pictures and graphics used on the Internet

hacker — a person skilled with computers and Internet use, who is therefore able to get into computer programs

HTML — *(HyperText Mark-up Language)* the computer code used to create web pages

hyperlink — addresses, words, or graphics that are inserted into documents on the world wide web (A click on the link leads to another web page.)

hypertext — a word or group of words that form a hyperlink

ISP — *(Internet Service Provider)* a company that provides connections to the Internet

keyword — a word that you type into a search engine

login or **logon** — to connect to the Internet

logoff — to disconnect from the Internet

lurking — reading messages in a newsgroup without posting any messages

mailbox — a place where the ISP keeps email for a user

net surfing — visiting sites on the Internet

offline — not connected to the Internet

online — connected to the Internet

post — to place a message in a newsgroup or discussion group so others can read it

search — to explore the Internet for information on a specific topic

search engine — program that searches for Web pages that contain specific words

server — a computer that provides an Internet service to clients

SPAM — *(Sending Particularly Annoying Messages)* junk email or postings in discussion groups

upload — to send files or information from your computer to another computer, usually through a modem or higher-speed connection

URL — *(Uniform Resource Locator)* the address for an Internet location

Web page — a computer document written in HTML code, placed for Internet access

Website — a collection of web pages set up by a person, group, or organization

World Wide Web — *(or the Web)* a huge collection of information that can be accessed by people all over the world through servers

MATH TERMS FOR EVERY OCCASION
Number Concepts & Relationships

Absolute Value — the distance a number is from 0 on the number line

Abundant Number — any number for which the sum of its factors (other than the number itself) is greater than itself

Additive Inverse — for a given number, the number that can be added to give a sum of 0. −4 is the additive inverse of +4 because −4 + (+4) = 0

Base — a standard grouping of a numeration system
(If a numeration system groups objects by fives, it is called a base 5 system; in a base 5 system, the numeral 23 means two fives and three ones.)

Cardinal Number — the number of elements in a set

Composite Number — a number having at least one whole number factor other than 1 and itself

Coefficient — the number amount in a mathematical expression
In the expression **5x**, **5** is the coefficient of **x**.

Digit — a symbol used to write numerals (In the decimal system, there are ten digits: 0, 1, 2, 3, 4, 5, 6, 7, 8, 9.)

Disjoint Sets — sets having no members in common
The sets {1, 9, 7, 12} and {3, 8, 11, 22} are disjoint sets.

Elements — the members of a set

Empty Set — a set having no elements, also called a null set
{ } or Ø represents an empty set.

Equivalent Sets — sets having the same number of members

Even Number — one of the set of whole numbers having 2 as a factor

Expanded Notation — the method of writing a numeral to show the value of each digit
5327 = 5000 + 300 + 20 + 7

Exponent — a numeral telling how many times a number is to be used as a factor
In 6^3, the exponent is 3
$6^3 = 6 \times 6 \times 6 = 216$

Finite Set — a set having a specific number of elements
{2, 5, 9, 15} is a finite set.

Inequality — a number sentence showing that two groups of numbers stand for different numbers
The signs ≠, <, and > show *inequality*.
7 + 5 > 12 – 9

Infinite Set — a set having an unlimited number of members

Integer — any member of the set of positive or negative counting numbers and 0
(. . . –4, –3, –2, –1, 0, 1, 2, 3, 4, . . .)

Irrational Number — a decimal that neither terminates nor repeats
Pi (≠) and most square roots are examples of *irrational* numbers.

Intersection of Sets — the set of members common to each of two or more sets

The intersection of these sets is 3, 7, and 8.

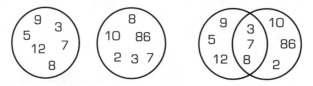

The symbol ∩ represents intersection.

Mixed Numeral — a numeral that includes a whole number and a fractional number, or a whole number and a decimal number

$7\frac{1}{2}$ and 37.016 are *mixed numerals*

Multiplicative Inverse — for any given number, the number that will yield a product of 1

$\frac{4}{3}$ is the *multiplicative inverse* of $\frac{3}{4}$ because $\frac{4}{3} \times \frac{3}{4} = 1$

Negative Integer — one of a set of counting numbers that is less than 0

Number — a mathematical idea concerning the amount contained in a set

Number Line — a line that has numbers corresponding to points along it

0 1 2 3 4 5 6 7 8

Numeral — a symbol used to represent or name a number

Numeration System — a system of symbols used to express numbers

Numerator — the number above the line in a fraction

Odd Number — a whole number belonging to the set of numbers equal to (n x 2) + 1
(Odd numbers are not divisible by 2.)
(1, 3, 5, 7, 9 . . .) are *odd numbers*.

Math Yellow Pages, Rev. Ed.

Opposite Property — a property that states that if the sum of two numbers is 0, then each number is the opposite of the other
–4 + 4 = 0; so –4 and 4 are opposites

Ordered Pair — a pair of numbers in a certain order, with the order being of significance

Ordinal Number — a number telling the place of an item in an ordered set (sixth, eighth, etc.)

Origin — the beginning point on a number line (the origin is often 0)

Palindrome — a number which reads the same forward and backward (121, 343, 5995, 87678, 91219, etc.)

Periods — groups of three digits in numbers

$$\underline{723},\underline{301},\underline{611}$$

millions period   thousands period   units period

Place Value — the value assigned to a digit due to its position in a numeral

Positive Integer — one of a set of counting numbers that is greater than 0

Powers of a Number — the number of times a number is multiplied by itself
This is indicated by a small, superscript number next to the main number.
10^4 means **10 x 10 x 10 x 10**

Property of One — a property that states that any number multiplied by 1 will equal that number

Property of Zero — a property that states that any number plus zero equals that number

Prime Factor — a factor that is a prime number
(1, 2, and 5 are **prime factors** of 20.)

Prime Number — a number whose only number factors are 1 and itself

Rational Numbers — a number that can be written as the quotient of two numbers
(A terminating or repeating decimal is rational.)

Real Numbers — any number that is a positive number, a negative number, or 0

Reciprocals — a pair of numbers whose product is one

($\frac{1}{2}$ and $\frac{2}{1}$ are reciprocals.)

Reciprocal Method — (for dividing fractions) a means of dividing fractions that involves replacing the divisor with its reciprocal, then multiplying

$$\frac{2}{3} \div \frac{4}{7} = \frac{2}{3} \times \frac{7}{4} = \frac{14}{12} = \frac{7}{6} = 1\frac{1}{6}$$

Rename — to name numbers with a different set of numerals
(592 can be renamed as 500 + 90 + 2.)

Roman Numerals — numerals used by the Romans for keeping records

Rounding — disregarding all digits in a number beyond a certain place value

Scientific Notation — a number expressed as a decimal number (usually with an absolute value less than 10) multiplied by a power of 10

$$4.35 \times 10^3 = 4350$$

Sequence — a continuous series of numbers ordered according to a pattern

Set — a collection of items called members or elements

Skip Count — counting by skipping a certain number of digits
(counting by 2's, 5's, and 10's, etc.)

Subset — every member of a set, or any combination of the members of a set

Union of Sets — a set containing the combined members of two or more sets

(The union of sets A and B is 7, 12, 14, 20, 25, 26.)

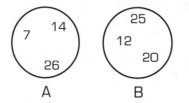

The symbol ∪ represents union.

Unit — the first whole number

Venn Diagram — a pictorial means of representing sets and the union or intersection of sets

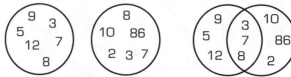

Whole Number — a member of the set of numbers (0, 1, 2, 3, 4 . . .)

Zero — the number between the set of all positive numbers and the set of all negative numbers

MATH TERMS FOR EVERY OCCASION
Operations & Computations

Addend — a number being added in an addition problem
In the equation **4 +7 = 11**, 4 and 7 are addends

Addition — an operation combining two or more numbers

Algorithm — method commonly used for performing computations involving mathematical operations (any computational procedure such as addition or multiplication)

Associative Property — (for addition and multiplication) the rule stating that the grouping of addends or factors does not affect the sum or product

$$(3 + 6) + 9 = 3 + (6 + 9)$$

$$(2 \times 4) \times 7 = 2 \times (4 \times 7)$$

Average — the sum of a set of numbers divided by the number of addends
The average of   1, 2, 7, 3, 8, and 9 =
$$\frac{1 + 2 + 7 + 3 + 8 + 9}{6} = 5$$

Binary Operation — any operation involving two numbers

Common Factor — a whole number that is a factor of two or more numbers
(3 is a factor common to 6, 9, and 12.)

Common Multiple — a whole number that is a multiple of two or more numbers
(12 is a multiple common to 2, 3, 4, and 6.)

Commutative Property — (for Addition and Multiplication) the rule stating that the order of addends or factors has no effect on the sum or product
3 + 9 = 9 + 3 and 4 x 7 = 7 x 4

Diagram — a 2-dimensional representation of an item or situation
Diagrams are often used to help with problem solving.

Difference — 1. the distance between two numbers on the number line;
2. the result of subtracting a lesser number from a greater number

In the equation **99 – 46 = 53**, 53 is the difference.

Distributive Property for Multiplication over Addition — the rule stating that when the sum of two or more addends is multiplied by another number, each addend must be multiplied separately and then the products must be added together
3 x (4 + 6 + 9) = (3 x 4) + (3 x 6) + (3 x 9) = 12 + 18 + 27

Dividend — a number that is to be divided in a division problem
In the equation **63 ÷ 7 = 9**, 63 is the dividend.

Divisibility — a number is divisible by a given number if the quotient of the two numbers is a whole number
(189 is divisible by 9 because 189 ÷ 9 is a whole number)

Division — the operation of finding a missing factor when the product and one factor are known

Divisor — the factor used in a division problem for the purpose of finding the missing factor
In this problem, the divisor is 12.

$$12\overline{)24} \quad 2$$

Equation — a mathematical sentence which states that two expressions are equal
7 x 9 = 3 + (4 x 15)

Estimate — an approximation or rough calculation

Factor — one of two or more numbers that can be multiplied to find a product
In the equation **6 x 9 = 54**, 6 and 9 are factors.

Factor Tree — a pictorial means of showing the factors of a number

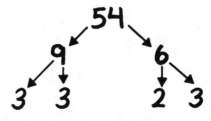

Greatest Common Factor — the largest number that is a factor of two other numbers
6 is the greatest common factor of 18 and 24.

Identity Element for Addition — 0 is the identity element for addition because 0 plus any given number equals that number.
3 + 0 = 3

Identity Element for Multiplication — 1 is the identity element for multiplication because 1 multiplied by any given number equals that number.
17 x 1 = 17

Least Common Multiple — the smallest whole number that is divisible by each of two or more given numbers
(The **least common multiple** of 2, 6, 9, and 18 is 18.)

Logic — "If–then" reasoning often used to solve math problems.
When using logical thinking, the problem solver thinks this way:
If x is true, then y must also be true.

Models — 3-dimensional replications of a figure or setting
Models are often used to help with problem solving.

Multiple — the product of two whole numbers

Multiplication — an operation involving repeated addition
5 x 4 = 4 + 4 + 4 + 4 + 4

Multiplicative Inverse — for any given number, the number that will yield a product of 1

$\frac{4}{3}$ *is the multiplicative inverse of* $\frac{3}{4}$

because $\frac{4}{3}$ *x* $\frac{3}{4}$ *= 1.*

Multi-step Problems — problems which take more than one step or more than one operation to solve

Open-Ended Problems — problems which have more than one correct answer
This is an open-ended problem:
What even, 3-digit numeral has digits whose sum is 12?

Prime Factor — a factor that is a prime number
1, 2, and 5 are prime factors of 20.

Product — the answer in a multiplication problem
In this problem, the product is 20,000.
40 x 5000 = 20,000

Quotient — the answer in a division problem
In this problem, the quotient is 75.
15,075 ÷ 201 = 75

Rename — to name numbers with a different set of numerals

Remainder — the number (less than the divisor) that is left after a division problem is completed
In this problem, the remainder is 6.

$$\begin{array}{r} 20 \\ 21\overline{)426} \\ -42 \\ \hline 6 \end{array}$$

Subtraction — the operation of finding a missing addend when one addend and the sum are known

Strategy — a method used to approach and solve a problem

Sum — the answer in an addition problem resulting from the combination of two or more addends

MATH TERMS FOR EVERY OCCASION
Fractions & Decimals

Common Denominator — a whole number that is the denominator for both members of a pair of fractions

For $\frac{3}{7}$ and $\frac{5}{7}$, 7 is a common denominator.

Common Factor — a whole number which is a factor of two or more numbers

3 is a factor common to 6, 9, and 12.

Common Multiple — a whole number that is a multiple of two or more numbers

12 is a multiple common to 2, 3, 4, and 6.

Complex Fraction — a fraction having a fraction or a mixed numeral as its numerator and/or denominator

$$\frac{\frac{1}{5}}{\frac{1}{3}}$$

Cross Product Method (or Cross Multiplication) — a means of testing for equivalent fractions

if $\frac{3}{5} = \frac{6}{10}$, then 3 x 10 will equal 5 x 6.

Decimal Numeral — a name for a fractional number expressed with a decimal point, such as .27

4.03 is a mixed decimal

Denominator — the bottom number in a fraction; the denominator tells how many parts there are in a whole unit

Equivalent Fractions — fractions that name the same fractional number

$\frac{3}{4}$ *and* $\frac{9}{12}$ *are equivalent.*

Fraction — the name for a fractional number written in the form $\frac{a}{b}$; a is the numerator, b is the denominator

Fractional Number — a number that can be named as a fraction, $\frac{a}{b}$. The numerator and denominator can be any numbers with the exception that the denominator cannot be 0.

Greatest Common Factor — the largest number that is a factor of two other numbers

6 is the greatest common factor of 18 and 24.

Improper Fraction — a fraction having a numerator equal to or greater than the denominator, therefore naming a number of 1 or more

$\frac{9}{4}$ *is an improper fraction.*

Math Yellow Pages, Rev. Ed.

Least Common Denominator — the smallest whole number that is a multiple of the denominators of two or more fractions

The least common denominator for $\frac{1}{3}$ and $\frac{3}{4}$ is 12.

Least Common Multiple — the smallest whole number that is divisible by each of two or more given numbers

The least common multiple of 2, 6, 9, and 18 is 18.

Like Fractions — fractions having the same denominator

$\frac{2}{9}$ and $\frac{12}{9}$ are like fractions.

Lowest Terms — When a fraction has a numerator and denominator with no common factor greater than 1, the fraction is in lowest terms.

$\frac{3}{7}$ is a fraction in lowest terms.

Mixed Numeral — a numeral that includes a whole number and a fractional number, or a whole number and a decimal

$7\frac{1}{2}$ and 37.016 are mixed numerals.

Numerator — the number above the line in a fraction

Percent — a comparison of a number with 100, expressed using the % symbol

45% is a comparison of 45 to 100.

Proportion — a number statement of equality between two ratios

$$\frac{3}{7} = \frac{9}{21}$$

Rate — a comparison of two quantities

Ratio — a comparison of two numbers expressed as $\frac{a}{b}$

Reciprocals — two numbers whose product is one

$\frac{1}{3}$ and $\frac{3}{1}$ are reciprocals because $\frac{1}{3} \times \frac{3}{1} = 1$.

Reduced Fraction — a fraction whose numerator and denominator are not divisible by any number other than 1

$$\frac{3}{7}$$

Repeating Decimal — a decimal in which a certain set of digits repeats without end

(0.363636)

Terminating Decimal — a decimal that shows a quotient of a whole number and a power of 10

$0.0204 = \frac{204}{1000}$ *$3.56 = \frac{356}{100}$*

Terms of a Fraction — the numerator and denominator of a fraction

MATH TERMS FOR EVERY OCCASION
Geometry & Measurement

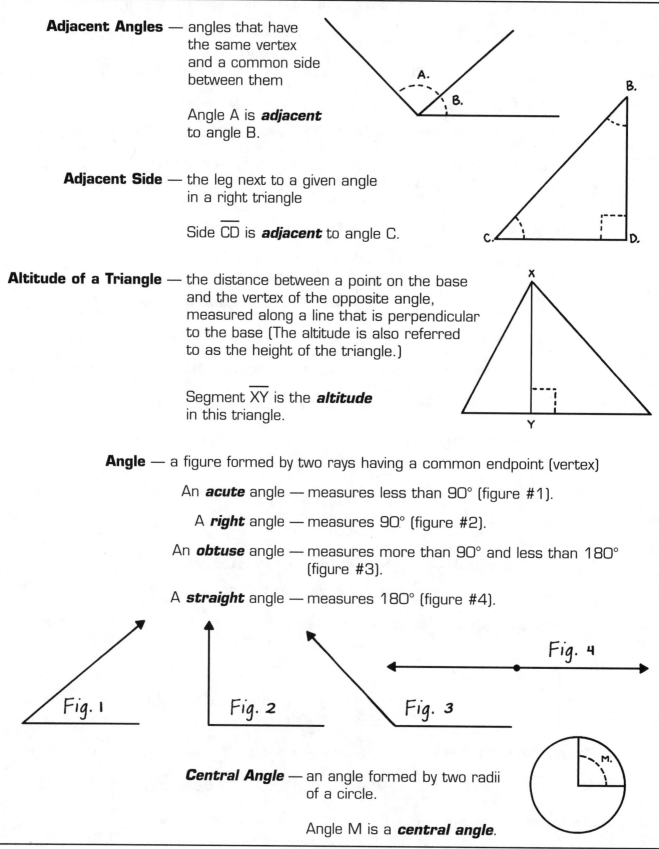

Adjacent Angles — angles that have the same vertex and a common side between them

Angle A is **adjacent** to angle B.

Adjacent Side — the leg next to a given angle in a right triangle

Side $\overline{CD}$ is **adjacent** to angle C.

Altitude of a Triangle — the distance between a point on the base and the vertex of the opposite angle, measured along a line that is perpendicular to the base (The altitude is also referred to as the height of the triangle.)

Segment $\overline{XY}$ is the **altitude** in this triangle.

Angle — a figure formed by two rays having a common endpoint (vertex)

An **acute** angle — measures less than 90° (figure #1).

A **right** angle — measures 90° (figure #2).

An **obtuse** angle — measures more than 90° and less than 180° (figure #3).

A **straight** angle — measures 180° (figure #4).

Fig. 1   Fig. 2   Fig. 3   Fig. 4

Central Angle — an angle formed by two radii of a circle.

Angle M is a **central angle**.

48

Angles, continued

Complementary Angles — two angles whose combined measurements equal 90°
X and Y are **complementary** angles

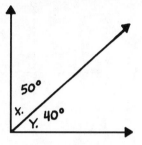

Congruent Angles — angles having the same measure

Corresponding Angles — angles that are formed when a line intersects
two parallel lines; corresponding angles are congruent.
B and F (below) are **corresponding** angles

Supplementary Angles — two angles whose combined measurements equal 180°
A and B (below) are **supplementary** angles.

Vertical Angles — angles that are formed opposite one another when two
lines intersect; vertical angles are congruent.
E and H (below) are **vertical** angles

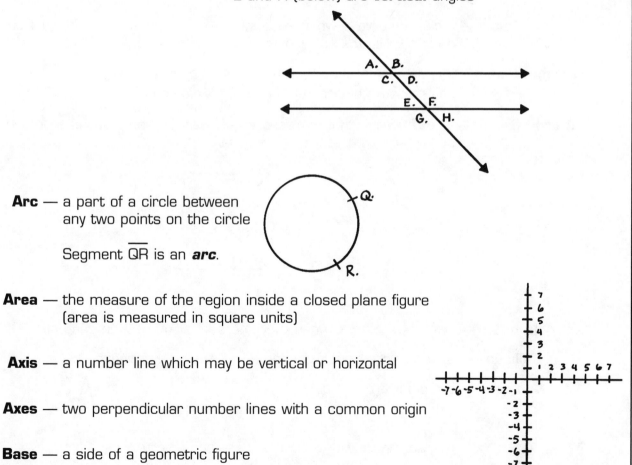

Arc — a part of a circle between
any two points on the circle

Segment $\overline{QR}$ is an **arc**.

Area — the measure of the region inside a closed plane figure
(area is measured in square units)

Axis — a number line which may be vertical or horizontal

Axes — two perpendicular number lines with a common origin

Base — a side of a geometric figure

Bisect — to divide into two congruent parts

Bisector — a line or ray that divides a segment or angle into two congruent parts

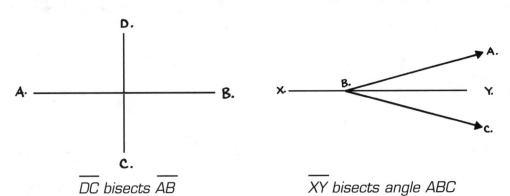

$\overline{DC}$ bisects $\overline{AB}$ $\overline{XY}$ bisects angle ABC

Capacity — the measure of the amount that a container will hold

Chord — a line segment having endpoints on a circle

$\overline{XY}$ is a chord.

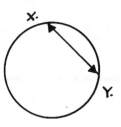

Circle — a closed curve in which all points on the edge are equidistant from a given point in the same plane (See circle above.)

Circumference — the distance around the outside edge of a circle
The measure of circumference = π x diameter

Closed figure — a set of points that encloses a region in the same plane; a curve that begins and ends at the same point

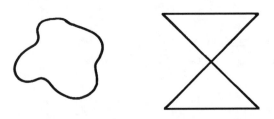

Coincide — Two lines coincide when they intersect at more than one point.

Collinear — When points are on the same line, they are collinear.

Compass — a tool for drawing circles

Cone — a space figure with a circular base and a vertex

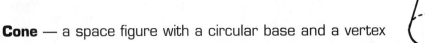

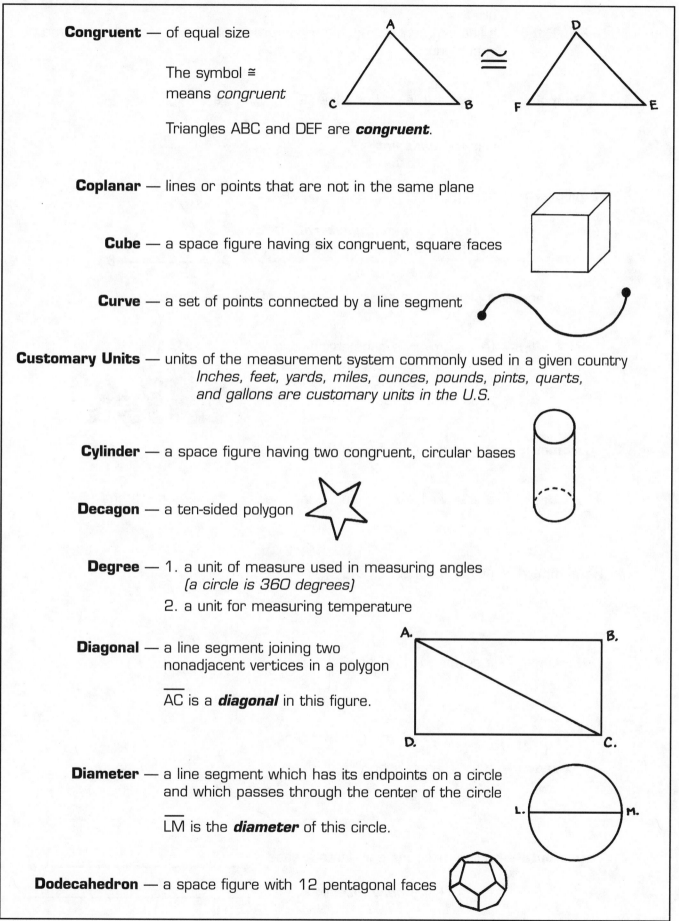

Congruent — of equal size

The symbol ≅
means *congruent*

Triangles ABC and DEF are ***congruent***.

Coplanar — lines or points that are not in the same plane

Cube — a space figure having six congruent, square faces

Curve — a set of points connected by a line segment

Customary Units — units of the measurement system commonly used in a given country
Inches, feet, yards, miles, ounces, pounds, pints, quarts, and gallons are customary units in the U.S.

Cylinder — a space figure having two congruent, circular bases

Decagon — a ten-sided polygon

Degree — 1. a unit of measure used in measuring angles
(a circle is 360 degrees)
2. a unit for measuring temperature

Diagonal — a line segment joining two nonadjacent vertices in a polygon

$\overline{AC}$ is a ***diagonal*** in this figure.

Diameter — a line segment which has its endpoints on a circle and which passes through the center of the circle

$\overline{LM}$ is the ***diameter*** of this circle.

Dodecahedron — a space figure with 12 pentagonal faces

Edge — a line segment formed by the intersection of two faces of a geometric space figure

Endpoint — a point at the end of a line segment or ray

G ●————————→

G is the *endpoint* of this ray.

Equilateral — having sides of the same length

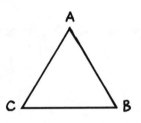

Figure ABC is an *equilateral* triangle. All of its sides are the same length.

Face — a plane region serving as a side of a space figure

Flip — to "turn over" a geometric figure

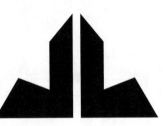

The size or shape of the figure does not change.

Geometry — the study of space and figures in space

Gram — a standard unit for measuring mass in the metric system

Hemisphere — half of a sphere

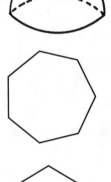

Heptagon — a seven-sided polygon

Hexagon — a six-sided polygon

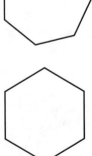

Horizontal — a line that runs parallel to a base

Line GH is a *horizontal* line.

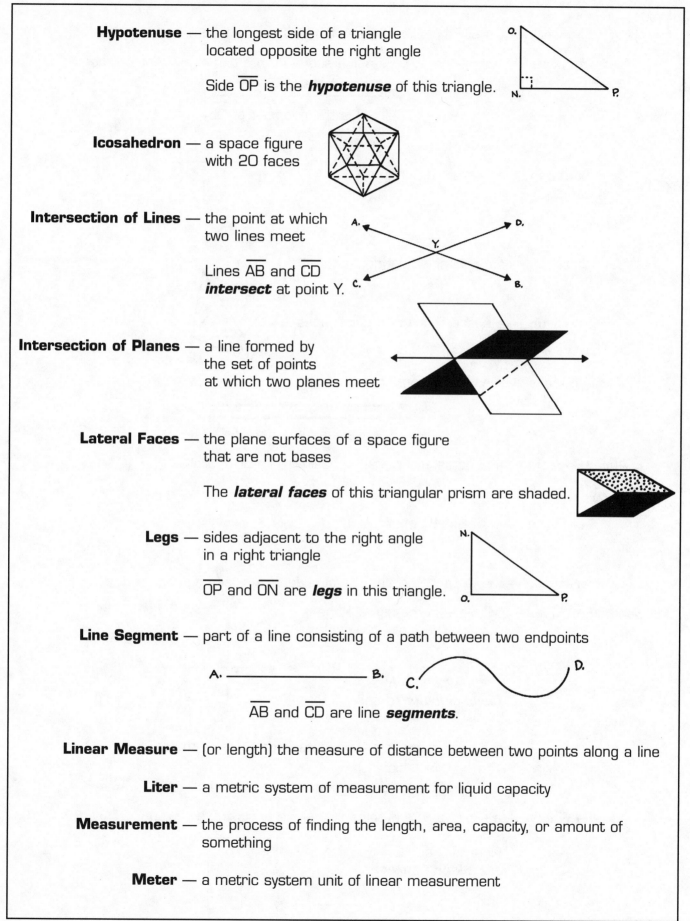

Hypotenuse — the longest side of a triangle located opposite the right angle

Side $\overline{OP}$ is the **hypotenuse** of this triangle.

Icosahedron — a space figure with 20 faces

Intersection of Lines — the point at which two lines meet

Lines $\overline{AB}$ and $\overline{CD}$ **intersect** at point Y.

Intersection of Planes — a line formed by the set of points at which two planes meet

Lateral Faces — the plane surfaces of a space figure that are not bases

The **lateral faces** of this triangular prism are shaded.

Legs — sides adjacent to the right angle in a right triangle

$\overline{OP}$ and $\overline{ON}$ are **legs** in this triangle.

Line Segment — part of a line consisting of a path between two endpoints

$\overline{AB}$ and $\overline{CD}$ are line **segments**.

Linear Measure — (or length) the measure of distance between two points along a line

Liter — a metric system of measurement for liquid capacity

Measurement — the process of finding the length, area, capacity, or amount of something

Meter — a metric system unit of linear measurement

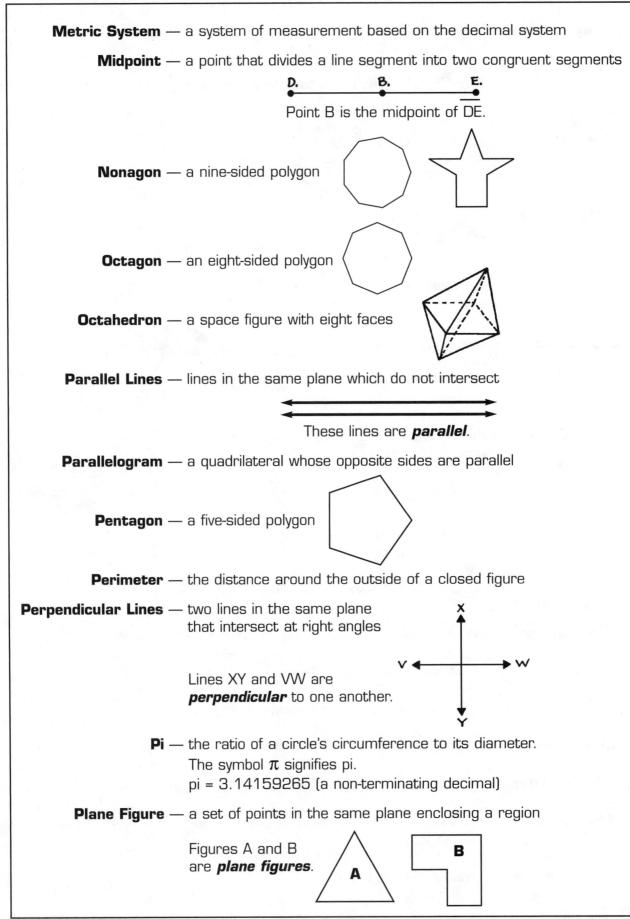

Metric System — a system of measurement based on the decimal system

Midpoint — a point that divides a line segment into two congruent segments

Point B is the midpoint of DE.

Nonagon — a nine-sided polygon

Octagon — an eight-sided polygon

Octahedron — a space figure with eight faces

Parallel Lines — lines in the same plane which do not intersect

These lines are *parallel*.

Parallelogram — a quadrilateral whose opposite sides are parallel

Pentagon — a five-sided polygon

Perimeter — the distance around the outside of a closed figure

Perpendicular Lines — two lines in the same plane
that intersect at right angles

Lines XY and VW are
perpendicular to one another.

Pi — the ratio of a circle's circumference to its diameter.
The symbol π signifies pi.
pi = 3.14159265 (a non-terminating decimal)

Plane Figure — a set of points in the same plane enclosing a region

Figures A and B
are *plane figures*.

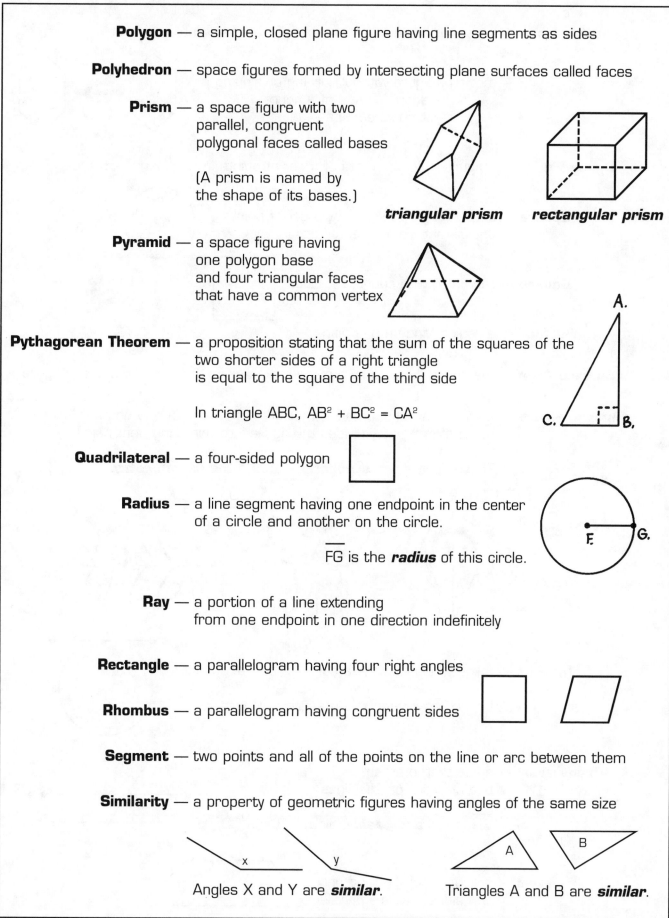

Polygon — a simple, closed plane figure having line segments as sides

Polyhedron — space figures formed by intersecting plane surfaces called faces

Prism — a space figure with two parallel, congruent polygonal faces called bases

(A prism is named by the shape of its bases.)

triangular prism　　*rectangular prism*

Pyramid — a space figure having one polygon base and four triangular faces that have a common vertex

Pythagorean Theorem — a proposition stating that the sum of the squares of the two shorter sides of a right triangle is equal to the square of the third side

In triangle ABC, $AB^2 + BC^2 = CA^2$

Quadrilateral — a four-sided polygon

Radius — a line segment having one endpoint in the center of a circle and another on the circle.

$\overline{FG}$ is the **radius** of this circle.

Ray — a portion of a line extending from one endpoint in one direction indefinitely

Rectangle — a parallelogram having four right angles

Rhombus — a parallelogram having congruent sides

Segment — two points and all of the points on the line or arc between them

Similarity — a property of geometric figures having angles of the same size

Angles X and Y are **similar**.　　Triangles A and B are **similar**.

Skew Lines — lines that are not in the same plane and do not intersect

Slide — moving a figure without turning or flipping it
The shape or size of a figure
is not changed by a slide.

Space Figure — a figure which consists of a set of points in two or more planes

Sphere — a space figure formed by a set of points
equidistant from a center point

Square — rectangle with congruent sides

Surface — a region lying on one plane

Surface Area — the space covered by a plane region or by the faces of a space figure

Symmetric Figure — a figure having two halves that are reflections of one another;
a line of symmetry divides the figure into two congruent parts

These figures are **symmetric**. ST is a line of **symmetry**.

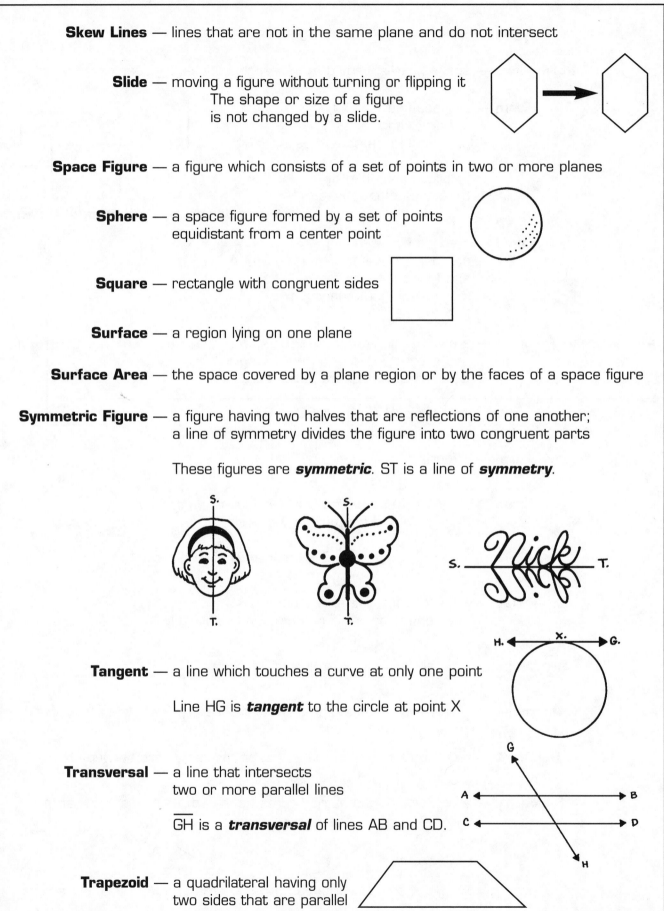

Tangent — a line which touches a curve at only one point

Line HG is **tangent** to the circle at point X

Transversal — a line that intersects
two or more parallel lines

$\overline{GH}$ is a **transversal** of lines AB and CD.

Trapezoid — a quadrilateral having only
two sides that are parallel

Triangle — a three-sided polygon

Acute Triangle — a triangle in which each of the three angles is less than 90°

Equilateral Triangle — a triangle with three congruent sides and three congruent angles

Isosceles Triangle — a triangle with at least two congruent sides

Obtuse Triangle — a triangle having one angle greater than 90°

Right Triangle — a triangle having one 90° angle

Scalene Triangle — a triangle in which no two sides are congruent

Turn — a move in geometry which involves turning, but not flipping, a figure

The size or shape of a figure is not changed by a turn.

Unit — 1. the first whole number
2. a determined quantity used as a standard for measurement

Vertex — a common endpoint of two rays forming an angle, of two line segments forming sides of a polygon, or of three planes forming a polyhedron

Point Z is the **vertex** of this angle.

Vertical — a line that is perpendicular to a horizontal base line

Line KL is **vertical**.

Volume — the measure of capacity or space enclosed by a space figure

MATH TERMS FOR EVERY OCCASION
Statistics, Graphing, & Probability

Average — the sum of a set of numbers divided by the number of addends
The average of 1, 2, 7, 3, 8, and 9 =
$$\frac{1+2+7+3+8+9}{6} = 5$$

Chance — the probability or likelihood of an occurrence

Combination — a selection of a set of things from a larger set without regard to order

Coordinate Plane — a grid on a plane with two perpendicular lines of axes

Coordinates — a pair of numbers which give the location of a point on a plane

Counting Principle — a way to find the number of possible outcomes of an event with multiple stages. The total number of possible outcomes is the product of the outcomes of each stage.

Data — figures, facts, or information

Dependent Events — two events in which the result of the first event affects the outcome of the second event

Event — a set of one or more outcomes

Frequency — the number of times a given item occurs in a set of data

Frequency Graph — a way to organize and picture data using a grid

Frequency Table — data arranged on a table to show how often events occur

Function — a set of ordered pairs of numbers that follow a function rule and in which no two first numbers are the same
{(2, 5) (3, 6) (4, 7) (5, 8) (6, 9)}
The rule for this set is to add one.

Graph — a drawing showing relationships between sets of numbers

Bar Graph — a graph that represents data with bars

Circle Graph — a graph that represents data by showing a circle divided into segments

Line Graph — a graph that uses lines to show changes in data over time

Grid — a set of horizontal and vertical lines spaced uniformly

Math Yellow Pages, Rev. Ed.

Histogram — a bar graph showing frequency data

Independent Events — events whose outcomes have no effect on later events

Interval — amount of space or time

Mean — average; the sum of numbers in a set divided by the number of addends

The *mean* of {6, 8, 9, 19, and 38} is $\frac{80}{5}$ or 16.

Median — the middle number in a set of numbers. The median is determined by arranging numbers in order from lowest to highest and by counting to the middle

The *median* of {3, 8, 12, 17, 20, 23, and 27} is 17.

Mode — the score or number found most frequently in a set of numbers

The *mode* of {36, 3, 12, 9, 7, 9, 23, 4, 12, 7} is 12.

Odds — the numerical likelihood of a chosen outcome in comparison to another

Odds Against — the numerical chance that an outcome will not be chosen; the ratio of unfavorable outcomes to favorable outcomes

Odds In Favor — the numerical chance that an outcome will be chosen; the ratio of favorable outcomes to unfavorable outcomes

Outcome — a possible result in a probability experiment

Permutation — an arrangement of data in a definite order

Pictograph — a graph that uses pictures or symbols to represent numbers

Prediction — the projection into the future of possible outcomes, based on data at hand

Probability — a study of the likelihood that an event will occur

Random — an experiment in which the results are not predictable, even when repeated

Range — the difference between the greatest number and the least number in a collection of data

Sampling — a method of gaining data from a selection of a larger amount of data, in order to make predictions about larger amounts

Statistics — numerical observations or data

MATH TERMS FOR EVERY OCCASION
Pre-Algebra

Absolute Value — the distance of a number from zero on a number line

Axes — the two perpendicular number lines in a coordinate plane that intersect at 0

Coefficient — the number value in a mathematical expression
In the expression **8x**, **8** is the coefficient of **x**.

Coordinate Plane — a grid on a plane with two perpendicular lines of axes

Coordinates — a pair of numbers that give the location of a point on a plane

Coincide — the intersection of two lines in more than one point

Collinear Points — points that lie on the same line

Coordinate — a number paired to a point

Coordinates — a pair of numbers paired with a point

Coordinate Plane — a grid on a plane with two perpendicular number lines (axes)

Cube Numeration — a number raised to the third power (8^3)

Equation — a mathematical sentence which states that two expressions are equal
$$7 \times 9 + 3 + (4 \times 5) = 86$$

Equivalent Equations — equations that have the same solution

Evaluate — to substitute a number for each variable in an expression and simplify the expression

Function — a set of ordered pairs (x, y) where for each value of x, there is only one value of y

Inequality — a number sentence showing that two numerals or two groups of numerals stand for different amounts or numbers
The signs < *(is less than)*, > *(is greater than)*, and ≠ *(is not equal to)* show inequality.
$$7 + 5 < 17 - 3$$

Integers — the set of numbers greater than and less than zero

negative integers — the set of integers less than zero

positive integers — the set of integers greater than zero

Math Yellow Pages, Rev. Ed.

Linear Equation — an equation whose graph is a straight line

Open Sentence — a number sentence with a variable

Opposites — two numbers on a number line that are the same distance from 0 on each side

Opposite Property — a property that states that if the sum of two numbers is 0, then each number is the opposite of the other
$$-4 + 4 = 0; -4 \text{ and } 4 \text{ are } \textbf{\textit{opposites}}$$

Ordered Pair — a pair of numbers in a certain order with the order being of significance

Radical Sign — the square root symbol $\quad \sqrt{}$

Rational Numbers — a number that can be written as the quotient of two numbers (A terminating or repeating decimal is rational.)

Real Numbers — any number that is a positive number, a negative number, or 0

Reciprocals — two numbers whose product is one

$$\tfrac{1}{3} \text{ and } \tfrac{3}{1} \text{ are } \textbf{\textit{reciprocals}} \text{ because } \tfrac{1}{3} \times \tfrac{3}{1} = 1.$$

Replacement Set — a set of numbers that could replace a variable in a number sentence

Solution Set — the set of possible solutions for a number sentence

Square Root — a number that yields a given product when multiplied by itself
The **square root** of 25 is 5 because 5 x 5 = 25

Scientific Notation — a number expressed as a decimal number (usually with an absolute value less than 10) multiplied by a power of 10
$$4.53 \times 10^3 = 4530$$

Solution — the number that replaces a variable to complete an equation

Variable — a symbol in a number sentence that could be replaced by a number
In $\textbf{\textit{3 + 9x = 903}}$, $\textbf{\textit{x}}$ is the variable.

X-Axis — the horizontal number line on a coordinate grid

Y-Axis — the vertical number line on a coordinate grid

FAST FACTS
Addition and Subtraction Facts Matrix

To find an addition fact: Locate one addend on the top horizontal row. Locate the second addend on the leftmost vertical row. Draw an imaginary line from each number to the box in which the lines meet. The number in that box is the sum of the two addends.

To find a subtraction fact: Locate one addend in the top horizontal row. Draw an imaginary line from that number down the page vertically until you come to the number from which you are subtracting. Draw an imaginary line from that number to the leftmost box. The number in that box is the missing addend.

+	1	2	3	4	5	6	7	8	9	10	11	12
1	2	3	4	5	6	7	8	9	10	11	12	13
2	3	4	5	6	7	8	9	10	11	12	13	14
3	4	5	6	7	8	9	10	11	12	13	14	15
4	5	6	7	8	9	10	11	12	13	14	15	16
5	6	7	8	9	10	11	12	13	14	15	16	17
6	7	8	9	10	11	12	13	14	15	16	17	18
7	8	9	10	11	12	13	14	15	16	17	18	19
8	9	10	11	12	13	14	15	16	17	18	19	20
9	10	11	12	13	14	15	16	17	18	19	20	21
10	11	12	13	14	15	16	17	18	19	20	21	22
11	12	13	14	15	16	17	18	19	20	21	22	23
12	13	14	15	16	17	18	19	20	21	22	23	24

Math Yellow Pages, Rev. Ed.

FAST FACTS

Multiplication and Division Facts Matrix

To find a multiplication fact: Locate one factor on the top horizontal row and the second on the leftmost vertical row. Draw an imaginary line from each number to the box in which the lines meet. The number in that box is the product of the two factors.

To find a division fact: Locate the divisor on the top horizontal row. Draw an imaginary line from that number down the page vertically until you come to the number being divided. Draw an imaginary line from that number to the leftmost box. The number in that box is the missing factor.

x	1	2	3	4	5	6	7	8	9	10	11	12
1	1	2	3	4	5	6	7	8	9	10	11	12
2	2	4	6	8	10	12	14	16	18	20	22	24
3	3	6	9	12	15	18	21	24	27	30	33	36
4	4	8	12	16	20	24	28	32	36	40	44	48
5	5	10	15	20	25	30	35	40	45	50	55	60
6	6	12	18	24	30	36	42	48	54	60	66	72
7	7	14	21	28	35	42	49	56	63	70	77	84
8	8	16	24	32	40	48	56	64	72	80	88	96
9	9	18	27	36	45	54	63	72	81	90	99	108
10	10	20	30	40	50	60	70	80	90	100	110	120
11	11	22	33	44	55	66	77	88	99	110	121	132
12	12	24	36	48	60	72	84	96	108	120	132	144